D0563737

You've Got a Friend

...one of the nicest things you can have,
and one of the best things you can be.

You've Got a Friend

...one of the nicest things you can have,
and one of the best things you can be.

photo-art by **MARK J. BARRETT**

WILLOW CREEK PRESS®

Published by Willow Creek Press, Inc.
P.O. Box 147, Minocqua, Wisconsin 54548

Design: Jackie J. Barrett
Printed in China

For you, my friend,
A small token...
...for words unspoken.

$\mathcal{A}$ friend
may well be reckoned
the masterpiece of nature.

~ Ralph Waldo Emerson

*Friendship isn't a big thing—
it's a million little things.*

~Author Unknown

A friend is one of the
nicest things you can have,
and one of the best things
you can be.

~Douglas Pagels

*Animals are
such agreeable friends—
they ask no questions,
they pass no criticisms.*

~George Eliot

$\mathcal{F}$riends are relatives
you make for yourself.

~Eustache Deschamps

Everyone hears what you say. Friends listen to what you say. Best friends listen to what you don't say.

~Author Unknown

𝓕riends are
those rare people
who ask how you are
and then wait for the answer.

~Author Unknown

*If I had to sum up
Friendship in one word,
it would be Comfort.*

~Terri Guillemets

*Yes'm, old friends
is always best,
'less you can catch
a new one that's fit to
make an old one out of.*

~Sarah Orne Jewett

*W*hat is a friend?
A single soul
dwelling in two bodies.

~Aristotle

She discovered with great delight that one does not love one's children just because they are one's children but because of the friendship formed while raising them.

~*Gabriel Garcia Márquez*

*T*his is my wish for you: Comfort on difficult days, smiles when sadness intrudes, rainbows to follow the clouds, laughter to kiss your lips, sunsets to warm your heart, hugs when spirits sag, beauty for your eyes to see, friendships to brighten your being, faith so that you can believe, confidence for when you doubt, courage to know yourself, patience to accept the truth, Love to complete your life.

~Winnie The Pooh (A. A. Milne)

I like her because she
smiles at me and means it.

~Anonymous

The entire sum of existence
is the magic of being needed
by just one other person.

~Vi Putnam

*S*trangers
are just friends
waiting to happen.

~Rod McKuen

*A*re you upset little friend?
Have you been lying awake worrying?
Well, don't worry... I'm here.
The flood waters will recede,
the famine will end,
the sun will shine tomorrow,
and I will always be here
to take care of you.

~Charlie Brown to Snoopy

$\mathcal{W}$e secure our friends
not by accepting favors
but by doing them.

~Thucydides

Only your real friends
will tell you when
your face is dirty.

~Sicilian Proverb

A good friend is cheaper than therapy.

~Author Unknown

*S*uccess keeps you glowing,
But, only Friends keep you going.

~Author unknown

My friend is nice.
We like to play
We play together every day.
We laugh and cry
And laugh again
Because, you see, we're
Friends
Friends
Friends!

~ Jane S. Zion

*S*ince there is nothing
so well worth having
as friends, never lose a
chance to make them.

~Francesco Guicciardini

*S*ometimes you put walls up
not to keep people out,
but to see who cares enough
to break them down.

~Socrates

*Friends can be said to
"fall in like" with as profound a thud
as romantic partners fall in love.*

~Letty Cottin Pogrebin

Depth of friendship does not depend on length of acquaintance.

~Rabindranath Tagore

*T*he most I can
do for my friend
is simply be his friend.

~Henry David Thoreau

*L*et us be grateful
to people who make us
happy, they are the
charming gardeners who
make our souls blossom.

~Marcel Proust

*T*here was a definite process
by which one made people into
friends, and it involved talking
to them and listening to them
for hours at a time.

~Rebecca West

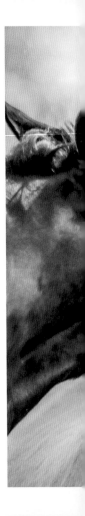

$\mathcal{I}$t's important to our friends
to believe that we are unreservedly
frank with them, and important to
the friendship that we are not.

~Mignon McLaughlin

*S*ilences make the
real conversations
between friends.
Not the saying but the
never needing to say
is what counts.

~ Margaret Lee Runbeck

*Shared joy is a double joy;
shared sorrow is half a sorrow.*

~Swedish Proverb

A mere friend
will agree with you,
but a real friend will argue.

~Russian Proverb

A friend accepts us as we are yet helps us to be what we should.

~Author Unknown

The most beautiful discovery true friends make is that they can grow separately without growing apart.

~Elisabeth Foley

It is by chance we met, by choice we became friends.

~Author Unknown

$\mathcal{W}$e are all travelers in the wilderness of this world, and the best we can find in our travels is an honest friend.

~Robert Louis Stevenson

$\mathcal{F}$riendship
is like a prism
through which
the many
variations
of beauty
are revealed
in our lives.

~Anonymous

No road is long
with good company.

~Turkish Proverb

riendship is a pretty full-time occupation if you really are friendly with somebody. You can't have too many friends because then you're just not really friends.

~Truman Capote

*Friendship is a very taxing
and arduous form of leisure activity.*

~Mortimer Adler

The essence of true friendship is to make allowance for another's little lapses.

~David Storey

A friend knows
the song in my heart
and sings it to me
when my memory fails.

~Donna Roberts

*The real test of
friendship is:
can you literally do nothing
with the other person?
Can you enjoy those moments
of life that are utterly simple?*

~Eugene Kennedy

We call that person who has lost his father, an orphan; and a widower that man who has lost his wife. But that man who has known the immense unhappiness of losing a friend, by what name do we call him? Here every language is silent and holds its peace in impotence.

~Joseph Roux

*C*lose your eyes
and think of me
and soon I will be there
To brighten up
even the darkest night.
You just call out my name
and you know wherever I am
I'll come running
to see you again...
You've got a friend.

~Carole King

$\mathcal{M}$ay you always have
love to share, health to spare,
and friends that care.